GASTON®

Goes to Texas

GASTON®
Goes to Texas

Written and Illustrated by JAMES RICE

By the Illustrator of
CAJUN NIGHT BEFORE CHRISTMAS®

PELICAN PUBLISHING COMPANY
Gretna 2008

First printing: November 1978
Second printing: September 1982
Third printing: September 1989
Fourth printing: March 1996
Revised edition: January 2008

Library of Congress Cataloging in Publication Data

Rice, James, 1934-2004
    Gaston goes to Texas.
    SUMMARY: Gaston the alligator gets hurled by a Louisiana hurricane into west Texas where he becomes the first alligator cowboy.
    [1. Alligators—Fiction. 2. Stories in rhyme]
I.   Title.
PZ8.3.R36Gar   [Fic]   78-12490
ISBN-13:   978-1-58980-531-6

Printed in Singapore
Published by Pelican Publishing Company, Inc.
1000 Burmaster Street, Gretna, Louisiana 70053

Designed by Gerald Bower

It was the season of autumn
    some five years ago,
In the Louisiana swampland
    a breeze began to blow.

It was born in the Gulf
    many miles south of land,
Where the waves gently swelled
    'til they pounded the sand.

And the tall cypress trees
    bent near to the ground,
In the terrible storm
    no calm could be found.

The creatures were routed
    from the swamp's quiet refuge,
There could be no escaping
    from the savage deluge.

Poor Gaston was lifted
    and blown through the air,
Over bayous and treetops
    far away from his lair.

'Til he dropped to the ground
    on a West Texas ranch,
Where no bayous meandered—
    just an alkali branch.

Three tall mounted cowboys,
    grizzled, dirty, and rough,
Started down from their saddles,
    O, my, they looked tough!

One shifted his body
    and spoke up with a grin,
"Howdy there, odd stranger,
    what a way to drop in!"

"We saw you a ridin'
    on that West Texas breeze.
Follow us to the ranch house
    and we'll put you at ease."

They fed Gaston and clothed him
    and treated him right,
And in Texas tradition
    put him up for the night.

They promised to teach him
    the skills of their trade,
The work would be rugged
    but he'd surely be paid.

Forty dollars a month,
    with beans on the side,
Twenty hours a day
    he'd rope and he'd ride.

Gaston wasn't ambitious,
    he'd never been paid,
He had spent all his time
    in a cool bayou shade.

But the cowboys insisted,
    they were friendly and warm,
To try it for a while
    would do him no harm.

Oh, what a strange sight
    in his full cowboy gear,
The old cowhands would laugh,
    when Gaston wasn't near.

He took up the challenge
    of the rough cowboy life,
From dawn until midnight
    his hours filled with strife.

He tried making a loop
    with a stiff rawhide rope,
But try as he might
    success seemed beyond hope.

Every morning 'fore daybreak
    he'd mount a cayuse,
Those stiff, jolting pitches
    would shake the kinks loose.

The cattle were longhorns,
   big, rangy, and lean,
There's no dumber critter—
   tough, hungry, and mean.

On horseback he'd chase them
    'cross the broad Texas plain,
He couldn't get near them,
    his efforts seemed in vain.

He would ride his mustang
    and throw out the rope,
But the cattle slipped through
    like wet bars of soap.

Gaston would turn one way,
    the longhorns the other,
He'd chase them all day
    'til he couldn't move further.

At the end of each shift
    he'd plop into bed,
With his saddle for a pillow
    to rest his tired head.

And the ground for a mattress
    to ease his stiff back,
He'd just close his eyes
        then—out of the sack!

One day followed the other,
    each was just like the last,
'Til they all came together
    and a full month had passed.

One day Gaston discovered
    to his utmost surprise,
He was no longer a greenhorn
    in the old cowhands' eyes.

He could now tame a mustang
   and drive a mean steer,
He could bulldog and rope 'em
   with no trace of fear.

He stayed on 'til roundup
   and branding was done,
Then went into town
   to have some good fun.

The cowhands loved Gaston
   and urged him to stay,
But he looked for his homeland
   and soon went on his way.

So, now deep in the swampland
a close search reveals
A friendly old alligator
who wears spurs on his heels.